CHEVROLET CORVETTE

Osprey AutoHistory

CHEVROLET CORVETTE

1968-82; 305, 327, 350, 427 & 454 V8s

THOMAS FALCONER

Published in 1983 by Osprey Publishing Limited
12–14 Long Acre, London WC2E 9LP
Member company of the George Philip Group

Sole distributors for the USA

Osceola, Wisconsin 54020, USA

© Copyright Osprey Publishing Limited 1983

This book is copyrighted under the Berne Convention. All rights reserved. Apart from any fair dealing for the purpose of private study, research, criticism or review, as permitted under the Copyright Act, 1956, no part of this publication may be reproduced, stored in a retrieval system, or transmitted in any form or by any means, electronic, electrical, chemical, mechanical, optical, photocopying, recording or otherwise, without prior written permission. All enquiries should be addressed to the Publishers.

British Library Cataloguing in Publication Data

Falconer, Thomas
   Chevrolet Corvette.—(Autohistory)
   1. Corvette automobile
   I. Title   II. Series
   629.2'222   TL215.C6
ISBN 0-85045-500-6

Editor Tim Parker
Associate Michael Sedgwick
Picture research by the author

Filmset in Great Britain
Printed in Spain

Contents

Chapter 1
1968–69; The new body *6*

Chapter 2
The chassis in service *25*

Chapter 3
1970–72; More and less power *41*

Chapter 4
1973–74; Years of choice *53*

Chapter 5
1975–77; The middle years *62*

Chapter 6
St Louis and Bowling Green *80*

Chapter 7
1978–79; Metamorphosis . . . *93*

Chapter 8
1980–82; . . . For a new age *109*

Notes on American model years *127*

Specifications *130*

Acknowledgements *133*

Index *134*

Chapter 1
1968-69; The new body

It doesn't seem like 15 years ago since the unforgettable day on which I first saw the new 1968 model Corvette. It was late September in 1967 and I was walking home from downtown Detroit; from the architect's office where I was working on the elevations of a new Ford truck assembly plant which was to be built in Louisville, Kentucky. It was just as stiflingly hot as it had been all summer but now the heat was combined with a strong breeze and the promise of one of the thunderstorms which mark the approach of autumn in the mid-western states. Now Detroit is prospering again and windy old East Jefferson Boulevard has even witnessed the Formula One Grand Prix of 1982. But then, in 1967, the city was still recovering from the shock of the terrifying riots. These I had witnessed for five sad days and nights earlier in the summer.

As I was walking east on East Jefferson, my first view was a distant one from behind and I was impressed, for even by the standards of the time, the Corvette was an absolutely dazzling car. GM styling was at one of its peaks, the 'Coke bottle' Pontiac range was into its third year, the Camaro and Firebird were well established and the Oldsmobile Toronado had a superbly styled body for GM's first front wheel drive production car. But I was still staggered by the impertinence of the stylist in fitting such a tiny tight-drawn convertible top to

1968–69; THE NEW BODY

emphasise the bunched shoulders of the rear wings over those wide, wide rear wheels.

The split back bumper was a nice carry over from the old style Corvette while the superbly incorporated Kamm-theory tail reminded me of the Ferrari 250GTO. Getting closer to that one car I noticed the car's shape from the side; I thought the nose was a bit too short but from the front it was devastating. The tiny one piece front bumper had to be the smallest attached to any American car for 30 years, and it fitted into a recess to smooth the body line further. I saw through the grilles that the headlights in their parked position apparently obscured half of the air intake, but actually the air was forced to the radiator through horizontal slots beneath the nose. These were backed by a tiny spoiler which actually served to increase the local

Corvette started out with a fibreglass body and six cylinder engine. In 1953 when only 300 cars were made the styling was remarkably advanced for its time. This is a 1954 model

CHAPTER ONE

1968–69; THE NEW BODY

By 1956 a V8 engine, and manual transmission had boosted sales sufficiently to justify a new model. Like all Corvettes ever built this 1957 had a fibreglass body

CHAPTER ONE

air pressure.

I later learned that although this might be an ideal aerodynamic and visual solution it was less than satisfactory in practice when a car was fitted with both the options of the Big Block engine and air conditioning. In the hotter parts of the States with the air conditioning on, there simply wasn't sufficient cooling air drawn through the air conditioning and engine cooling radiators and this led to engine over-heating problems. In Northern Europe, of course, this was never really a problem and overheating 427s usually had something worse wrong with them.

I took in more of the car. Further up the long nose, after the concealed headlights and over a sensual power bulge, the bonnet or hood finished in two full width panels. The first was a casting and

Having gained four headlights in 1958 the Corvette was restyled for 1961 with a new sleeker tail. Basically similar for 1962, this would be the last year for at least two decades that the Corvette was offered with an externally accessed luggage boot

1968-69; THE NEW BODY

slotted for its full width and the second fitted flat onto the windscreen glass with no rubber seal and, what's more, no windscreen wipers! At last, a dream car was in production and those worst excesses of the triumph of the practical over the beautiful—wipers—were hidden beneath a lifting panel.

I remembered that in Bulgaria they used to take their wiper blades off and store them in the car because they would be stolen, while in California

In 1963 a radically different chassis with all round independent suspension was introduced under a new and shorter body. The chassis would not be significantly modified for another twenty years. This is a 1966 327 convertible

CHAPTER ONE

Opposite top *A windy afternoon in Detroit September 1967, first sighting of the new Corvette*

Opposite bottom *A passer by was persuaded to hold the author's camera to record the momentous event*

Below *1963–67 models were available in convertible or coupe form, this is a 1967 coupe*

they took them off just to prove their faith in the endless summer, but now good old General Motors had outdone them all and banished them to a secret black space where sunshine could never perish them.

I was more and more impressed as I searched over the whole car. Like any enthusiast I wanted to learn more. Research began and this book is part of my findings. I was a Corvette buff there and then.

This superb aerodynamic wiper cover was subsequently but immediately criticized by the American journals; in practice it works extraordinarily well. When the wiper switch is turned on in the cockpit a vacuum ram is energized and lifts the flap on parallelogram hinges. When it is fully raised, a switch operated by the ram at its full travel completes the circuit to the wiper motor, and the

CHAPTER ONE

Michigan has now joined the growing list of states who do not require front licence plates

two speed wipers are in action. In keeping with all Corvettes ever made, the wipers bow politely to each other rather than keeping parallel as on the majority of European cars. Left alone, the wiper flap system works for years without maintenance and most of its problems stem from meddling with the instrument panel and stereo, or repairing crash damage.

Like most of its contemporaries from the design studios at Warren, that new Corvette had managed to lose its side vent windows, a feature which exists on most cars as much to simplify the window lift

1968-69; THE NEW BODY

mechanism for the designer as to give any decent ventilation to the driver. Only the '63 to '67 series Corvettes had them, but they had provided the easiest access for car thieves. Now they would find a less damaging entrance by prying out the rather flexibly mounted glass.

That convertible was available with an optional hard top which was a particularly attractive design. Though almost impossible for one man to remove and replace, it was fixed at eight positions for a snug fit and had polished metal caps at its extreme rear corners to enable it to be stored when not in use on a

GM press shot of the 68 coupe interior. Ignoring the obvious differences to the production car, note the 68 only door panels, large steering wheel, pillar mounted interior lamp and ignition switch on dash. Contrast this view with the 1978 interior on page 103

CHAPTER ONE

1968–69; THE NEW BODY

timber or concrete floor or against a wall without sliding. I have always felt that Corvette designers were Corvette drivers and this sort of practical detail confirms my view. Mounted on the car, the hard top seems to sit lower than the coupe body, and its rakish rear glass window inspires a feeling of greater interior space than one would find in the vertical back windowed coupe. This spaciousness is an illusion though, especially if the soft top is still folded down inside the car. It can however, be removed easily and stored for winter by undoing four bolts from their captive nuts.

Of course, seeing the 1968 production Corvette 'in the metal' for the first time was a tremendous and unforgettable experience. It would be quite wrong though, to suggest that it was a complete surprise.

In fact I had been primed by the most elegant of marketing techniques, the use of the dream car. The principle is simple and has been used by all the Big Three Americans over the last 30 years and in particular by Chevrolet previously for the '53 and '63 Corvettes. First you show a dream car with impossible curves, fantastic gadgetry and a general air of impracticality for everyday road use, and then two years later you introduce something that looks very similar as a production car. The advantage of the system is that the new production shape does not need to be sold cold but has already halfway captured the imaginations of the buying public.

But I was surprised as to just how much of the Mako Shark dream car, displayed at London's Earls Court Motor Show in the autumn of 1965, had been incorporated. It was a production car I was looking at. It shared not only the same chassis as the dream car, for that had been based on a 1965 Corvette, but also the external doorpulls built into the curve of the wing at the back of the doors, the flip up cover for the windscreen wipers and the wheel openings stretched out to emphasise the width of the tyres.

The United States was at war in 1968 and thousands of American service men in South East Asia dreamed of coming home to a Corvette. This coupe has its roof panels in and the optional wheel covers

1968–69; THE NEW BODY

Inside, the new model shared with the 'marketing version' the fibre optic light bulb failure warning system, that projects the actual glow of each individual bulb around the car, into a display panel in the seat divider panel on the console.

The dream car had been a fixed head coupe. In addition to the convertible I was examining on East Jefferson, a new coupe had been introduced. It incorporated a full, steel roll cage with a T-bar and detachable fibreglass roof panels. These have always been remarkably wind and water tight when properly adjusted and shimmed. Removed from storage and protected from scratching in the vinyl bags provided, they take up much of the useable space behind the seats where a strap is provided to secure them. In 1977 GM briefly offered a kit to go with the official luggage rack, but it was then withdrawn almost immediately because the panels tended to become unhooked from the rack and fall in the road at high speed. Not until 1980 was another system offered to store the removed roof panels externally. To extend the 'convertible coupe theme further, the small vertical back window was made removable and storage provided in a drop-down rack on the luggage area ceiling. This meant that the rear window defroster had to be of a fan type incorporated in the left hand rear pillar, instead of the usual heating wires.

The convertible version of the car came with a totally concealed soft top which could be lowered with one hand while moving at city traffic speeds. The convertible is certainly my favourite type, giving the sensation of fresh air motoring which T-roof can never achieve. Indeed, driving a Corvette fast with the top down is as rewarding as riding a powerful motorcycle without the necessary restrictions of Barbour suit, gloves, boots and helmet.

The 1969 cars incorporated a number of improvements rendering them more desirable than '68s.

Opposite *Wide wheels upset the Corvette's straight line ability and overstress rear wheel bearings. This 1968 convertible has the optional hard top fitted, Telegraph Hill, San Francisco 1968*

CHAPTER ONE

The 1969 ZL1 is the rarest of all Corvettes, only two produced and only one with impeccable documentation. This is Wayne Walker's car, note the factory side pipes and factory striping

Though it is perhaps irrelevant now, there was a tremendous purge on quality control at the St Louis assembly plant to get rid of some of the rattles and poor finish of which many owners of the 1968 cars complained.

This latest restyled Corvette has been constantly improved ever since its introduction. Improvements were made to the seats to give better support, a map pocket was incorporated in the dash in front of the passenger, and the outside door handles were made fully functional discarding the separate push buttons used on 1968s. Along with a far more convenient column mounted ignition and steering lock switch, an optional tilt/telescopic steering wheel was made available. The old 16 in. 1963 to 1967 steering wheel which also found its way onto the

'68s was changed for a smaller diameter 15 in. wheel on the 1969.

Another new feature which, curiously, most owners of '69 to '70 cars are unaware of is the headlight washing system. Water jets spray the outer (dipped) beams when the windscreen washer switch is depressed and the headlights are in the raised position.

The wheel width was increased to 8 in. using the same trims as the '68 and these wheels would remain the standard Corvette equipment for the next 13 years.

In 1969 the name Stingray reappeared on the side of the car, a name which was not used on the car or in advertising during 1968. The previous series of cars which had shared the same chassis from '63 to '67 had used the name but as two words, Sting Ray. The single word Stingray script was used every year

Bill Mitchell with the Mako Shark and a 1968 coupe

CHAPTER ONE

Geneva Salon 1968. Rare European show appearance

until the end of 1976. It has to be conjecture, but I believe the name was reintroduced at the insistence of Bill Mitchell, the then brilliant head of GM styling, who had come up with the name after catching such a fish. The name was first used on the 1959 Chevrolet racer privately entered by Bill Mitchell and driven by Dick Thompson. Bill Mitchell finally left General Motors in 1976 and it is significant that the Stingray name disappeared at the same time. It is not a name that slides easily off the American tongue, and automotive marketing men take even these subtleties seriously.

The engine line up for 1968 had been carried over almost intact from 1967. On the 1969s the Small

1968–69; THE NEW BODY

Block engine was given a larger stroke from $3\frac{1}{4}$ to nearly $3\frac{1}{2}$ in. to make it into the 350 which still powered the 1982 line. The base 350 had 10.25:1 compression ratio and the optional 350 hp version was 11:1. There were no less than 6 of the Big Block 427 engines from the basic L-36 390 hp to the legendary cast iron L-88 and aluminium block ZL-1. The sheer acceleration of the big block engines is astonishing but for normal driving the Small Block is my favourite. It handles much better because of its reduced weight, is more willing to rev, is quieter and most important today it is much more economical. Normal fast daily driving with both automatics and manuals, easily gives 20 miles per Imperial gallon.

1968 L-88 beneath the front bumper

CHAPTER ONE

1968 was the last year for the four tail lights with separate reversing lights under the rear bumper. Certainly the later cars have a cleaner arrangement with the inboard lights serving as reflectors and reversing lamps, but there is still something wonderfully clever about those four bright tail lights cruising towards a Pacific sunset.

The rear lights for 1969 had stop, tail and brake with a dual filament bulb behind a red lens for the outboard pair and a white reversing lens within a larger reflector for the inboard pair. This arrangement gave a red rear direction indicator, something not seen on European cars since the late 1950s.

The most popular conversion in Europe is to replace all the rear lights with those from the first series Opel Manta with their outer trims removed. A method widely used on Australian Corvettes and on British right hand drive conversions is to change the reversing light lens to amber, and wire these up as indicators, whilst they also remain as amber reversing lights.

The 1969 door panels were introduced to give more shoulder room, and did this admirably; with their long arm rest area and integrated door handles they looked good too, but unfortunately, the production process adopted was not up to GM's usual high standard. They were made from cardboard, foam and a heat formed vinyl sandwich, but they stretched the vinyl thinnest at the point of maximum flexure and abrasion at the top of the arm rest! They deteriorated quickly. While these are readily available from after-market suppliers, they are expensive, and it is now rare to find a '69–'77 with original panels in perfect order.

Already it must be obvious, the '68 Corvette looks were captivating—and here to stay. A new Corvette high time was ahead. I'm happy to say I suspected so on East Jefferson in September 1967.

Chapter 2
The chassis in service

The 1968 Corvette chassis was inherited without any changes from the 1963–67 series. It is a fully boxed perimeter frame with five crossmembers. On manual cars the gearbox crossmember is welded into position and on automatics it's removable to enable the Turbo-Hydramatic to be removed without disturbing the engine. This crossmember also has two holes which carry the twin exhaust pipes towards the back of the car. The pipes are swept together underneath the differential to avoid contact with the transverse spring at full extension. Immediately ahead of the rear wheels the perimeter rail is turned up vertically and then sweeps back to support the fuel tank and rear bumper. In 1969 extra reinforcement fillets were introduced to brace this by the front of the trailing arm.

The pressed and fabricated trailing arms mount on a pair of rubber bushes into the kickup, where, unfortunately, they are subject to all the spray from the road wheels, making these bushes the hardest to replace on the car in service. The differential is mounted on its own separate crossmember which in turn mounts to the higher part of the chassis with two very effective vibration absorbing bushes. The front suspension is by unequal length wishbones or A-arms and is very similar to the rest of the contemporary Chevrolet passenger car line. The perimeter frame rails sweep in ahead of the doors to

CHAPTER TWO

pick up the attachments for the upper and lower arms.

If a Corvette is crashed at the front, the lower A-arms and inner bushing pins are the first to suffer, but then unfortunately the curve on the frame rail will be the next to bend, and this is the first place to look on a car for signs of accident damage. Mild impact damage can be straightened out on a realignment rig, but more severe cases which actually crease the boxing at this point necessitate replacement of the whole chassis. Side or rear impacts usually damage the trailing arms, which are easily replaced, and damaged caused by side impacts to the wheels, being absorbed by the

Corvette with body removed, engine, drive line, suspension and fuel tank in position

Passenger side view of the chassis showing the sharp kick-up over the rear suspension and the 18 gallon fuel tank, mounted less than ideally for good weight distribution

trailing arms, rarely affects the chassis which is extremely strong at this point. Oblique impact to the rear crossmember is easily straightened.

There can be few cars on which the chassis frame is as easy to replace as it is on a Corvette. The body is fixed to the chassis at eight points with each of the bolt heads being well protected from the elements. Removal of the body is simplicity itself given an adequate hoist or preferably two. The exercise is really essential if, say, the fuel lines are to be replaced in their true positions or a full restoration undertaken. It is unusual for a Corvette chassis to be damaged by rust. In spite of being inadequately painted at the factory the steel is of good quality, proper gauge and well ventilated.

While it's generally accepted that the Corvette has been the best handling of all American front-engine rear-wheel drive cars for many years—mainly because it is the only one with independent rear suspension—it is obviously going to fall short when compared to much more expensive exotic cars, usually from Europe. The suspension keeps the tyre tread parallel to the ground only over a

CHAPTER TWO

The small block Chevrolet engine mounted in a Corvette. Note that there is stainless steel shielding around distributor, wire and plugs to prevent radio interference with the fibreglass body

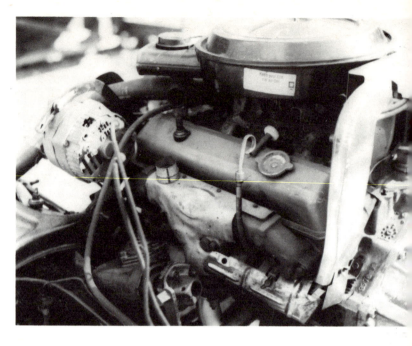

very limited range of the full suspension travel, so wide wheels and tyres cannot be used on the car without upsetting the handling.

To be driven fast the Corvette needs to be handled sympathetically. Driven hard through a medium speed bend some vagueness and initial understeer is soon followed by roll oversteer. After the suspension has taken up the roll the car then understeers again as the corner continues. Lifting the accelerator in the middle of a bend results in strong oversteer.

A number of kits are available to control these symptoms, and since all the basics are in the car in the first place it can be made to handle well with only bolt-on modifications. It may be that the symptoms are purposely designed in to manifest themselves at those relatively low speeds so that home market owners, who are used to cars which don't handle at all by European standards, are not

THE CHASSIS IN SERVICE

Independent rear suspension 1968–79, differential is mounted directly to the chassis via rubber isolated cross-member. Note gusset reinforcements to chassis introduced in 1969. Drive shafts from upper link of the suspension parallelogram, rubber bushes in lower link lead to poor location during hard cornering

1980–82 Aluminium differential and cross-member

CHAPTER TWO

inspired to corner too fast for their own safety!

From 1968 to 1972 70-profile crossplies were fitted, then replaced by 70-profile steel-belted radials from 1973 onward. When wider tyres had to be used for circuit racing then suspension travel has to be drastically reduced. In spite of all the above the Corvette is still tremendous fun to drive fast through bends of all types.

Any car is designed to provide satisfactory performance and freedom from problems for the first owner and first few years of its life only. This is particularly true of high performance cars and the manufacturer is naturally concerned with selling the car only to the man who buys it new. Second and subsequent owners buy for a fraction of the cost, and thus are faced with more repair bills and expensive and sometimes scarce spare parts.

The Corvette is a contradiction in this way. Its

Aluminium cased four-speed transmission in the 1977 car shifts less sweetly than the old Muncie box, phased out in the mid seventies. Gear lever is mounted direct to chassis to prevent gear shift rattle common on 1963–67 cars. This car has full dual exhaust fitted, GM engineers admit privately that this modification is worth some 25 bhp

high resale value reflects its quite extraordinary durability and resistance to corrosion when compared to other such cars. The easy availability and comparative cheapness of parts is taken for granted by many Corvette owners and certainly these factors have always contributed to the appeal of American cars in Europe.

The great majority of all Corvettes have been fitted with Small Block Chevrolet engines, possibly the most popular car engine ever made in various displacements of 265, 283, 305 and 350 cu. in. In 1969 the 350 replaced the 327 which had been the Corvette Small Block since 1962.

Treated carefully and regularly serviced, a Small Block is good for at least 150,000 miles. The 427 and 454 Big Block engines don't seem to have the same longevity, perhaps because their owners feel more need to demonstrate their astonishing power more often. The durability of the boxed steel chassis with fibreglass body is outstanding. It deteriorates only as a result of crash damage in temperate climates. While there are few cars which will outlast it, the Corvette does have some characteristic faults and too many buyers have found out too late what these are.

The worst problem concerns the cast iron brake calipers with their four pistons. Introduced in 1965 for the last three model years of the old style Sting Ray, they were modified for 1967 to remove the first headache—corrosion behind the hard plastic insulator between disc pad and piston. This had been very sensibly incorporated to prevent heat from the pad boiling the fluid, but had been found unnecessary in normal road use. Corrosion of the aluminium piston forced the insulator to crack and break off, allowing road dirt and water past the outside dust boot which is also retained.

Unfortunately, this modification was inadequate, as not only does water penetrate and rust the

CHAPTER TWO

1977 Corvette with centre section back in position. Corvette owes its good weight distribution (47 per cent front/53 per cent rear) and its lack of leg room to its engine being mounted well behind the front axle line. Notice how far out the energy absorbing bumper system projects tubular cross member doubles as vacuum reservoir for flip up headlights

polished bores of the cast iron caliper from the outside, but moisture also reaches the bores from the inside. What apparently happens is that the brake fluid itself absorbs the water from the atmosphere, being hygroscopic and this water rusts the bores and corrodes the aluminium pistons. I have seen it suggested that there are additional chemical problems due to the aluminium alloy brake pistons speeding up the corrosion of the cast iron, but I am not a chemist! The result of this corrosion is that the air is drawn past the seal which no longer has a polished seat and leads to the spongy brake pedal feel experienced by Corvette owners the world over.

This kind of corrosion takes about four years to mature, and as I write in 1982, the owners of 1978 cars are reporting this problem. Even when the

calipers are badly rusted, fluid does not necessarily pour down the inside face of the wheels and tyres and the caliper can look quite dry externally. Air will however, still be drawn into the system either when the brake pedal is released after application, or as a result of the pumping action of a slightly out of true brake disc or loose wheel bearing.

It would be easy to criticize GM for not avoiding this inherent problem, but such criticism would be unfair, as they are such superb brakes in every other way apart from their rather high unsprung weight. The manufacturer would surely, rightly point out, that if the brake fluid is changed regularly, say every two years from new, then corrosion will never appear. Silicone based brake fluid is now available which is nonhygroscopic.

Once discovered, the solution might seem to be a set of new calipers, pistons and seals, but in 1976 an American after-market manufacturer set up the tooling to bore the calipers, and sleeve them with highly polished stainless steel. These are made available on an exchange basis at a fraction of the cost of new units. Since then a number of manufacturers in the States have joined the field and the price has come down with the competition. Even so, at 1982 prices it is still costing about £400 per car to change all the calipers.

A chapter of possible Corvette woes can easily finish at this point since the other problems are comparatively minor and cheap to rectify. None of them in itself should prevent a potential Corvette owner from buying his dream car, though a combination of them may do so.

Another weak point of the braking system is the parking brake. This operates by a conventional pull up hand-lever mounted in the console between the seats, rather than by the foot operated pedal found on most American cars. It actuates a separate internally expanding shoe and drum system, the

CHAPTER TWO

Most parts can be interchanged on any Corvette from 1968–82. This Florida enthusiast built his ideal by fitting 1974 convertible top and rear deck, a 1970 454 engine and 1969 factory side pipes to his otherwise stock 1980. Its not really even customising, the factory sticker on the air cleaners says 'Keep your GM car all GM'!

CHAPTER TWO

454 engine in a 1980 'composite convertible'

drum being on the inside of the back brake disc. As the drum is only $6\frac{1}{2}$ in. in diameter it is never going to be a very efficient system. Its operation is through levers and adjusters which are cheap steel stampings without proper bushes, and these seize up and rust in service. Because the caliper and brake disc must be removed to do all but the most simple adjustments, this part of the car is ignored by most owners.

The same manufacturers who make the stainless steel calipers are now manufacturing stainless components for the handbrake and these really do solve the problem by being corrosion free.

Immediately adjacent to the rear hand brake mechanism is the third regular Corvette problem and that is the rear wheel bearings. They must be dismantled for lubrication and as doing both sides can be a full day's job with nothing to show for it at the end except a strong feeling of self righteousness and a big service bill, then this essential procedure (which should be done, in my view, every 25,000 miles), is often forgotten. Once the bearings dry up, what starts as a small squeak can develop into a flopping rear wheel and a rear disc grinding into its caliper within 25 miles. A very ingenious plastic greaser is available which enables greasing to be done by removing only the drive shaft and forcing grease through the outer bearing to the inner. If this is done regularly and the bearings are within tolerance, then the owner need never discover how awful a rear wheel bearing collapse can be on the road.

Once a bearing has collapsed, or if the spindle needs to be pulled out for any other reason, it will be found that the bearings are a very tight press fit onto the spindle and into their housings. Thus it is usually beyond the home mechanic to extract them without damaging the fine thread on the end of the spindle. After new bearings have been fitted suc-

CHAPTER TWO

cessfully, the whole job must be repeated immediately to achieve the correct shimming between the two bearings. Anyone contemplating a long Continental trip in a Corvette should ensure that his rear wheel bearings are in order and properly lubricated before anything else, since this problem can occur without prior warning and be extremely hard to cure without the right parts and tools. The craze for extra wide wheels on Corvettes is happily fast disappearing: these exacerbated the situation because of the extra eccentric load imposed on the bearings.

Provided their fluid is changed every 50,000 miles and topped up only with TQ Dexron, both the Turbo-Hydramatic 350 and 400 automatic transmissions will outlast almost everything else on the car. On manual transmission cars the '68 to '74 Muncie gearboxes (so named because they were built at the GM gearbox plant at Muncie, Indiana) give bearing and synchromesh trouble only after very high mileages. The most usual symptom is jumping out of second gear while the car is on the over-run. Clutch life is 15–30,000 miles depending on usage. Further back in the transmission system the differential is immensely strong though the inner gear case will not take the strain of drag racing on sticky tyres.

The usual problem with the differential sounds much worse than it really is, and does not occur on pre-1970 cars unless they are fitted with the Positraction limited slip type, optional until then. The symptoms are a violent banging noise felt through the whole car at 2 to 5 miles an hour in forward or reverse or when negotiating low speed corners, all this when the differential is hot after a good long run. This is caused by the Positraction plates binding rather than sliding smoothly over each other. (The limited slip differential was an option until 1970 when it became standard.) A

THE CHASSIS IN SERVICE

1968 L-88 427

1981 engine and chassis, notice the stainless exhaust manifold and that troublesome caliper

couple of oil changes when hot, each time adding GM additive number 1052358, seems to cure the problem, though in severe cases the plates may need to be replaced.

Apart from replacement of normal service items the only other components on the mechanical side to give more than their fair share of problems are the needle roller bearing universal joints in the rear drive shaft which not only transmit all the power from the engine but form an essential link in the rear suspension.

Normal servicing is extremely simple. Like most American V8s, the small block has a tiny oil capacity of about a gallon required to refill, including the new filter. Apart from the 1970–72 LT-1 solid lifter engine all Small Block Corvette engines from 1968 to 1982 have automatic hydraulic valve adjustment, with the added bonus of preventing over revving. All models since 1975 have electronic ignition, so that with no valve or contact breaker clearances to check and adjust and only nine greasing points, all at the front end, the Corvette actually requires less work for a routine servicing than a Ford Cortina or even Chevrolet's Citation. On the home market the advantages to the Corvette owner are even more pronounced.

Of rival cars, Porsche, Ferrari, Maserati and Jaguars E type and XJ-S, none are as easy and cheap to maintain. Most of these have bodies made of a material which seems, to the Corvette owner at least, to be hilariously inappropriate—steel!

Chapter 3
1970-72;
More and less power

For the 1970 model year a number of refinements were made to the exterior of the car which made it look more expensive and better contrived. The cheap plastic front grilles of the previous two years with their small round parking lights were replaced with generous and expensive die cast elements; full size parking light lenses were built into either end.

The front marker lights were repositioned and enlarged to match the new front grille treatment. To go with the new grille die cast side vents, also of egg-crate pattern were fitted. Incidentally, this was the first side grille since the mid sixties which hadn't aped a Ferrari original. This one was inspired by the old Mercedes-Benz 300SL!

At the rear, dramatic new square exhaust outlets were fitted on the ends of the existing silencers in matching recesses under the rear bumpers. While they looked tremendous they were subject to rapid corrosion. Polished stainless steel replicas are, however, now available from aftermarket suppliers. in 1969, the wider eight inch wheels had protruded beyond the wheel openings and thrown road grit up the body sides. Now for 1970, the backs of both front and rear wheel openings were carefully turned out to protect the paintwork.

Under the bonnet, the 427s were increased to 454 cu. in. (7442 cc) by increasing their stroke a quarter-inch and were redesignated as LS-engines The LS-5

These GM press release photographs of the new 1970 actually show the 1969 model retouched to look like a 1970. The front and side grilles and new exhaust outlets have been painted in by hand. The artist has omitted the major difference for 1970, the extended flares behind the front and rear wheels to protect the body sides

CHAPTER THREE

At Felton drag strip, Northumberland, England a 1970 LS-7 454 with dual plate clutch and heavy duty brake option. The Corvette independent suspension gives excellent traction under these circumstances. Five-slot aluminium dish wheels were fashionable at the time, but drowned front brake discs in heavy rain. July 1974

delivered a staggering 500 lb ft of torque at 3400 rpm. The LS-7 of which only a few were made, developed 465 bhp. Sharing the high rise 454 bonnet was a new high revving, high horsepower LT-1 Small Block 350; this had mechanical as opposed to the normal hydraulic pushrods, and delivered 370 horsepower at 6000 rpm. It had a high rise aluminium inlet manifold topped by a Holley carburettor, and an 11:1 compression ratio. With the petrol available in America today these engines suffer from detonation and running-on but will still operate without these problems on the higher octane European petrol provided that points and timing are adjusted

1970–72; MORE AND LESS POWER

1972 model had flares behind wheel openings, continued for next 12 years

CHAPTER THREE

1970–72; MORE AND LESS POWER

absolutely right. The LT-1 featured contrasting stripes around the bonnet bulge, with 'LT-1' transfers.

Inside, the car was given new seats yet again, slightly lower to improve headroom and with an unlatching button high up at the back. Shoulder belts now passed through slots in the seats. A new de-luxe interior was also offered with leather seats and cut pile rather than loop carpet. This was extended up to the front half of the door trims and edged with a metal moulding. The centre console around the gear shift lever received a wood-grain trim. The radio loud speakers were moved from their muffled position in the foot wells to an acoustically ideal placement on either end of the top dash pad and thus reflected sound off the hard windscreen. They give an ideal stereo picture from this position, and can be heard even at high speed.

The 1971 was an almost exact carry over of the 1970 in external appearance. Indeed, to have

Opposite *Small bonnet bulge on 350 cu. in. car, wipers completely hidden below vacuum-operated flap*

Vacuum lifted twin $5\frac{3}{4}$ round headlights snap up instantly on pulling headlight switch. Driver has override control to leave lights off but up when required

Compare the different treatments of 1972 coupe and convertible. Snug fitting convertible top is completely hidden under rear deck when down

LT-1 was the solid lifter 350 produced 1970–72. High rise alloy manifold necessitated the use of the 454 bonnet with painted pinstripes and LT-1 transfers. These are now much sought after

1970–72; MORE AND LESS POWER

facelifted the perfection of the 1970 would have been a shame. The threat of the 2½ mph Federal-requirement bumpers all round was now a certainty, with 5 mph type at the front to follow. So the stylists left well alone and were working to adapt the Corvette for the future. Indeed, at this time many people though Corvette production would end in 1975 because of the requirements imposed by the barrier impact tests, and that GM management would take the easy way out.

Most of the world's makers were affected during the 1970s by the Federal emission requirements,

either because they also exported cars to the US, or because legislators in other countries didn't want to be left out of the fun, and the chance to gain votes from the environmental lobbies. The first round of US anti-pollution laws had forced the fitting of AIR pumps to many Corvettes since 1966, but compression ratios remained high and performance was virtually unaffected. After 1971 compression ratios had to come down to below 9.0:1, and this is reflected in the line of engines available. Also introduced at this time was controlled fuel tank ventilation which involves a lot of extra pipe work, a canister and loss of tank capacity, but no loss of performance.

For 1972 engine options continued as before, but factory horsepower was expressed in the new

Opposite *1972 454 coupe. Radial tyres were still not factory fitted!*

A Canadian registered 1970 coupe in England in 1972. Car with dealer-fitted Chevrolet luggage rack, is missing its rear Corvette letters. Fibreglass pod protects drop-down spare wheel

CHAPTER THREE

Society of Automotive Engineers (SAE) terms, rather than Gross as in previous years. This was in response to the road safety lobby, and marked the official end of the supercar era at GM. Under the Gross horsepower test method an engine was run without its air cleaner, exhaust system, radiator fan, alternator, and carburettor heater. Mixture and timing were adjusted for maximum power. For the SAE test the engine is tested as installed in the car with its proper air cleaner, exhaust system, silencers and radiator fan. All emission equipment is installed and the mixture and timing adjusted to meet the emission requirements. There were slight performance reductions on all three available engines. The 8.5:1 base engine was re-rated to 200 horsepower from 270, the 9.0:1 LT-1 engine came down from 330 Gross to 255 SAE, and the LS-5 454 Big Block from 365 to 270 horsepower.

The optional anti-theft alarm which was triggered by switches in both door pillars and the bonnet became a standard feature, and the fibre optic light bulb monitor system was dropped for ever.

After 10 successive years of soft bumpered production, the chrome bumpered cars with their tight radii seem to set off the well painted curving surfaces of the body to perfection, while the egg crate metal front and side grilles, larger front parking lights and marker lights and square cut exhaust outlets of the '70–'72s give a better proportions than on the 1968–69 Corvette. These are the Corvettes for sunny Sundays in summer and the collectables of the future!

Chapter 4
1973-74;
Years of choice

At the time the 1973 Corvette did not appear radically different from the '72, apart from its new plain side vents and, of course, the new plastic covered Federal front bumper. But in retrospect, it is clear that this was the turning point, the beginning of the new age for Corvettes, a change of emphasis for a changing world that had been properly perceived and comprehended by GM management. In America and Europe vast sums were being spent on freeways and motorways to connect the major cities, which were themselves being surrounded by beltways, ring roads, by-passes and *peripheriques*. Now the majority of driving was to be done on multi-lane highways with smooth running cloverleaf intersections. Thus the massive acceleration that had been so important for overtaking on two and three lane roads was ceasing to be as vital as it had been to the driver in a hurry.

Now the requirement was for silent travel on the new freeways and a better ride over all those expansion joints. The Corvette was to change from an agressive thrusting sports car to a quiet, long legged, mile eating personal cruiser. The 1973 Corvette incorporated some of the necessary modifications. The most important was a new system of body mounting with cushioned mounts, which, combined with thicker insulation under the carpets and sprayed-on sound deadener was quite astonish-

CHAPTER FOUR

1973 350 coupe (in background 1974 and 1958 convertibles). This is the favourite of many enthusiasts who like the long nose and chrome-bumpered tail. Radial tyres were new for 1973

ingly effective in reducing road transmitted noise. The new body mounts were a combination of rubber and metal bush which could be fitted to earlier cars to achieve the same kind of ride quality. Simultaneously, steel belted radial tyres were introduced as standard equipment with all the advantages of wet road grip, reduced rolling resistance and longevity which we now associate with this kind of tyre. It is, of course, unwise to run *any* Corvette with crossply or bias belted tyres on today's roads. Protests were made at the time about the extra noise and lower ultimate dry road grip of radials. The only reason that they weren't fitted before was simply lack of domestic supply in the large sizes required.

In 1968 most General Motors cars had hide-away wipers of the type pioneered in the mid '50s on the Citroën DS, tucked into a trough behind the bonnet.

Now the Corvette was made to comply and after five years the brilliant vacuum flap system was no more. Nevertheless, the engineers were still having fun in this area – since they had to retool for a new shape of bonnet they gave it a larger bulge and a full fresh air duct system to draw cold air from the high pressure area at the base of the windscreen. The plenum chamber in the bonnet is sealed to the air cleaner with a rubber flap mounted on the cleaner, and under light throttle openings air is still drawn from the engine compartment. But when the throttle is pressed sufficiently hard to activate the

GM, press release shot of 1973 coupe. Optional 8-slot aluminium wheels were quickly withdrawn, relaunched in 1976. Removing one roof panel is ideal for driving in winter sunshine. This prototype '73 has wrong nose badge, production badge is same as 1974

CHAPTER FOUR

1974 350 coupe

second chokes on the carburettor, a switch under the pedal activates a solenoid at the back of the bonnet, which in turn opens a flap and feeds the engine direct from the base of the windscreen. I wonder if there is any measurable power gain with this system, but the great thing about it is the quite fabulous noise created by bringing all that induction roar up to the base of the windscreen. On full throttle, particularly with the roof panels out or the convertible top down, the sound effect resembles that of a famous Italian twelve cylinder.

The new nose used ingenious energy dissipating

1973-74; YEARS OF CHOICE

draw bolts to absorb the Federal front barrier impact. While on close examination the detail design is not as crisp as on the previous year's cars the effect from a distance was to make an already long nosed car look longer than ever. For those who liked the new soft nose and the traditional aggressive spoilered tail with its chrome quarter bumpers, the 1973 model has the magic combination.

Another change towards the quiet, long distance cruiser was the abandonment of the removable back window which must have been the most rarely utilised of all Corvette features. With this gone

1974 dealer postcard

1973–74; YEARS OF CHOICE

Opposite *1974 convertible, soft-top up. Mirrors are not correct for Corvette*

1974 convertible. The sharp angles of the optional hardtop emphasise the Corvette's curves. Notice carb air inlet vent at rear of bonnet, Astro-ventilation vents in rear deck and '74 only plain filler cap cover and split rear bumper

CHAPTER FOUR

1974 convertible

there was improved noise and draught sealing and the end of one source of leaks, but best of all an increase in available luggage space because the drop down storage compartment in the ceiling of the luggage area could now be omitted.

1974 was the year of the Federal rear bumpers and the only year when the legislators insisted on the starter circuit being integrated with the seat belts, preventing its operation unless belts were fastened. The test of the truly original 1974 is to find the seatbelt starter interlock still working perfectly, but most of the interlocks were by-passed as permitted when the law was changed in 1975.

The Federal rear bumper was to become a feature of all Corvettes from now on; the soft panels painted in body colour gave a new and characteristic appearance to these cars. The 1974 rear bumper was the cleanest ever devised and was fitted only that year. Possibly for manufacturing reasons, it was split into two parts with a central split and was a beautifully clean shape which contrasted with the 1975–79 single-piece version with its ugly black over riders. To complete this clean and monochrome end image even the exhaust outlets were hidden.

The 1974 had no badge on its petrol filler cap, the only year this happened. 1974 was also the last year when you could open the filler cap and actually see with your own eyes how much petrol was in the tank. It was the last year too of the big block engine, available only in a low compression but still fairly high torque form, delivering 380 lb ft at 2800 rpm. When chief engineer Zora Arkus Duntov was asked by *Motor Trend* to name his favourite Corvette he named a red 1974 T-roof big block automatic, a car that could cross the American continent at $2\frac{1}{2}$ times the legal maximum speed in comfort and quiet. He obviously meant it; when I met him for lunch in November 1982 he was driving a blue 1974 454!

With the 55 mph speed limit now rigorously enforced the Corvette proved to have another outstanding virtue. Because of its fibreglass body, back-tilted radiator and concealed headlights behind angled covers, it has a less detectable radar image than any other American car. Indeed *Car and Driver* in a recent feature on 'stealth' cars found that the standard police radar would only start to detect a Corvette at a point half as close to it as it could detect a Honda Civic!

Chapter 5
1975-77; The middle years

The front and rear bumpers were revised again for 1975 and, presumably under pressure from the marketing department, small fake overriders painted black were moulded into the reshaped front bumper cover. This last modification was better integrated into the body by cutting its centre section back into the bodywork, and thus eliminating the harsh break line. At the rear, fake overriders were also incorporated in the cover which concealed the bumper, now featuring the hydraulic rams common to most other GM cars. This one-piece rear bumper had the advantage of losing the '74s split line, but was more expensive to repair. These rear covers only get damaged at one side or the other, and now the whole moulding had to be purchased.

There were also changes in the engine compartment and to the exhaust. A new high energy ignition system with magnetic triggering was introduced to fire the new clean mixtures required by the emissions regulations. Much worse, the dual exhaust was routed into a single catalytic converter approximately under the passenger seat, and then through a corrosion prone Y-piece back into the dual exhaust. The effect on the power output was as bad as might be expected, although the cleaner mixtures did help fuel economy. Fortunately, GM were kind enough to leave two holes in the cross

1975 coupe from the Isle of Man. Soft bumpers have small black painted overriders

CHAPTER FIVE

1975 coupe rear deck. Fibreglass construction makes production of this complex shape easy

member to enable the exhaust system to be converted back to an unrestricted dual, and this second hole remained in the chassis until the 1980 model year. An L-82 engine had been introduced as the high performance replacement for the solid lifter LT-1 in 1973, and for 1975 a car fitted with the option now had L-82 badges on the bonnet. This L-82 was now to be the only optional Corvette performance engine until terminated at the end of 1980. It incorporated some quite exciting bits and pieces, including a forged crankshaft, shot peened rods and 9.0:1 impact extruded pistons. It also had a rejetted Quadrajet and some very attractive cast aluminium valve covers with polished fins.

It varied from year to year, but on average this high performance L-82 engine gave an extra 35 bhp, and at higher revs than its sister L-48, but with some loss of bottom end torque. This extra power is hard won considering the specification of the engine,

1968 427 L-88 coupe, complete with optional red stripe tyres

GM publicity shot of 1968 coupe with roof panels out and the optional wheel covers much favoured by the stylists at the time. But they were out of step with the deep, dished look that was to be the fashion for the next decade

Above *In 1969 the Corvette was still futuristic so the GM artists put a dream of the future into this background. Now the International Expo style looks more dated than the car*

Left *1969 427 L-88 convertible, note the optional bright insert to the side vents. Incredibly fast and desirable!*

Above left *1974 coupe at an English Lake District Corvette Rally*

Below left *1972 350 coupe in an English country lane. Corvettes are the unofficial ambassadors of the American motor industry abroad*

Left *Last of the small back windows, a 1977 in a leafy Baltimore suburb*

Above *In 1979 the front air dam, rear spoiler and glass roof became optional on any Corvette*

Right *The 1978 Limited Edition Pace Car replica*

Rear view of the 1978 Silver Anniversary Corvette. Celebrating the 25th Anniversary of Corvette production, Silver Anniversary was the first full two tone car ever offered and came with a number of options as standard including aluminium wheels

Above *Fifteen years on, the $25,000 collector's edition with electronic fuel injection, finned aluminium wheels and a frameless glass hatchback*

Right *1980 Corvette was the most streamlined yet*

particularly when some nice 10.5:1 compression pistons in an L-48 and some good British high octane petrol will deliver a lot more power far more cheaply! Such is the cost in performance terms of reducing octane rating.

1975 was the last year for convertibles and the Corvette managed to be one of the last such bodies produced in America. In 1968 more than half the cars produced were soft-tops but by 1974 they accounted for less than one seventh of total production and in the 1975 model year only 4629 were made, as against 33,836 coupes. The safety legislators had been threatening to outlaw them with roll over strength regulations, but these never materialized. The convertibles just disappeared

1975 engine bay. All cars now had 350 engines. Rubber seal around air cleaner mates to plenum chamber in bonnet. 1975 was last year for this feature. Air injection reactor (AIR) pump is ahead of air cleaner, air conditioning pump beyond

1975 coupe. Firestone 500 radials occasionally lost treads at high speed and were withdrawn from sale

CHAPTER FIVE

8-slot aluminium wheels became a 'regular production option' in 1976, reduced unsprung weight

anyway. Since almost all cars are built to order the low production level of roadsters reflected a lack of demand. It also emphasized again the change from traditional sports car to 'personal' car. The loss of these ragtops was particularly sad because the soft bumpered look suited the convertible so well, the softer body mounts reduced the squeaks and rattles that afflict open Corvettes more than coupes, and with its steeply raked windscreen, well protected low seating position and powerful heater, the later convertible is one of the most rewarding open cars to drive.

The 1976 car was much the same as the '75 with the substitution of a four spoked steering wheel borrowed from the lowly Vega compact saloon. This was at least smaller than the previous 15 in. thin rimmed three-spoke design which had been used since 1969, but was only destined to remain on the car for one year. Omitted from the rear deck of the car was the pair of air vent grilles and the bonnet also lost its splendid fresh air induction system. Instead, a plastic duct was run across the top of the radiator to draw cold air directly from the front of the car. The virtue of this system is that it made the bonnet lighter to open. 1976 also saw the end of the blower fan for rear window demisting, and the substitution of conventional heating elements.

A steel floor was fitted to 1976 Corvettes, replacing the fibreglass unit used previously. Chevrolet claimed at the time that this was to reduce heat and noise from the catalytic converter penetrating to the passenger compartment. While the use of this material must reduce the corrosion resistance of the car, seven years later I have yet to see a rusty floor. At the back of the car a new Corvette badge with

GM 1976 postcard showed new optional wheels

1975 coupe with luggage carrier, this car has later aluminium wheels fitted

italic lettering in one piece replaced the previous design which has eight individual letters.

A new option became available for '76, four aluminium wheels of an eight spoke slotted design, added up to a saving of 35 lb unsprung weight and looked terrific. They had been offered previously in 1973 but no sets were ever actually fitted by the factory and the option had been withdrawn. They were the same width as the standard steel wheels but have proved to be of remarkably high quality, resisting corrosion much better than most after market wheels of the same material.

The 1977 model-year cars were introduced with marketing material which again emphasized the change in Corvette character – from hard running sports car to fast and comfortable freeway cruiser. The engine line-up remained the same, but a new group of centre instruments in a new console was announced with a standard size radio aperture which permitted a whole range of radios and tape players to be ordered. At last, too, there was an illuminated pointer against the P-R-N-3-2-1 indicator for cars fitted with automatic transmission. As mentioned previously, the Stingray name was dropped and now the car was to be known only as a Corvette. Also new was a smart three spoke steering wheel with a colour co-ordinated leather sponge covered rim, the best Corvette steering wheel ever. The de-luxe interior was now standard and contrasting interior colours such as white leather seats and door panels with green carpets, door kicks and instrument panel started to become commonplace. Cloth seats were offered as an alternative to leather which was now standard.

Power steering and power brakes were now standard equipment and streamlined sports mirrors were offered for the first time. It was no longer necessary to engage reverse gear or 'Park' before the ignition key could be removed, a feature first introduced in 1969.

A new steering column was fitted to bring the headlight dip-switch up from the floor and the wiper control from the dashboard onto the column stalks, which also incorporated the switch for the cruise control, optional with automatic transmission. The interior light was removed from the back of the luggage compartment to the roof. The handbrake lever was now incorporated in a much improved seat divider console with a padded top; this was also higher than the previous hard plastic design and makes a far better arm rest. Externally the Stingray name was gone from the side of the wings, and on early production 1977 cars this area was as bare as it had been on the '68. Later in the year an elongated pair of Corvette crossed flags were added to match a new crossed flag badge on the nose of the car.

Chapter 6
St Louis and Bowling Green

General Motors is a big corporation making millions of motor vehicles every year and Chevrolet is its largest car manufacturing division. Components for Chevrolet cars are made in most of the 50 states; there are car assembly plants all over the North American continent.

More than 6000 Chevrolet dealers are able to sell new Corvettes and they buy them from Chevrolet along with Camaros, Impalas and the rest of the passenger car line. Spare parts for the cars are distributed to these dealers via eight parts warehouse centres and distribution plants across the country. These warehouses are supplied, in turn by the various component manufacturers. They are not supplied by the assembly plant itself which is only concerned with putting together complete cars.

In recent years interest in all Corvettes and their restoration has grown to such an extent that specialist shops have started selling just Corvette parts. Though some of these turn over millions of dollars a year and keep far more Corvette parts than a normal Chevrolet dealer, they all have to buy their GM parts from the dealer network. When parts become scarce for cars that are 10 or more years old, then small manufacturers start to reproduce them and sell through the specialist Corvette shops. These dealers often sell the majority of their stock by mail order and can be found not only in the continental United States but in Hawaii, Canada, Australia, England, Sweden, Germany and Switzerland as well. Since most of these foreign shops buy direct from Chevrolet dealers in the United States, they usually undercut the prices from the official GM dealers in their own countries.

In spite of all the reproduction parts available Corvette enthusiasts have a special reverence for genuine GM units. Discontinued GM spares in their original boxes are known as new old stock (NOS) and command prices at auto jumbles or swap meets that are far in excess of the price of reproductions.

GM Tech Centre of Warren, Michigan, where all General Motors cars are designed. White building in foreground is the new wind tunnel, which is big enough for a truck and semi-trailer. Between that and the lake is the styling building. Styling Dome, used for presentation, is to the left

Milford, Michigan, GM proving ground. More than 4000 acres in area and with 123 miles of road this is where most of the Corvette road testing is done. Inset Milford in the 1920s

GM parts are usually packed in strong white cardboard boxes with blue and black printing, which makes them a pleasure to handle.

Just why one of the world's largest manufacturers should bother to make an almost handbuilt sports car that over 30 years has averaged less than 25,000 units per year has always been something of a mystery. Certainly, the Corvette enthusiast is the last person to complain; he is perhaps frightened that the 'General' hasn't noticed what's been going on in those assembly plants in St Louis and now Bowling Green, and might just decide to stop the whole business!

The Corvette becomes a complete car for the first time on the production line at the assembly plant. American car production has long moved away from the Henry Ford principle of putting iron ore in at one end of the factory and driving cars out of the other. Just a brief look at the labelling on a random selection of Corvette spare parts shows that they

GM Assembly Division, Bowling Green. This aerial photograph of the new Corvette plant was taken in spring 1981. Railway siding and finished car despatch area to the left, office to the right

CHAPTER SIX

St Louis, the Corvette assembly plant 1954–81. A body taking shape on the birdcage

originate from all over North America, both from GM plants and from independent manufacturers. Stingray badges of the 1969 to 1976 cars come from Canada, along with many specialist plastic mouldings such as the rear storage compartment tray. Optional aluminium wheels are made in Mexico and the Big Block engines used to carry the label 'built by Chevrolet Tonawanda, the Number One team'; The Tonawanda engine plant is near Buffalo, New York. Although the fibreglass body is bonded together from its component parts at the assembly plant, these individual elements have all come in from a specialist manufacturer outside.

Corvettes are actually designed at the General Motors Technical Centre at Warren, a spectacular modern complex the size of a small town, partly designed by Eero Saarinen in 1955. Warren is an outer suburb of Detroit, traditional home of the American car industry. Prototypes are tested and developed at the GM test track at Milford, Michigan and the parts for the production cars are sent from all over America to be assembled by General Motors Assembly Division (GMAD).

Corvette assembly was at St Louis, Missouri from December 1953 to July 1981 in a plant which also assembled full size Chevrolet sedans and pick-up trucks; it was originally built in the 1920s to make wooden car bodies. Those were the days when the car companies bought and operated whole forests for the production of their bodies. This was a fascinating plant to visit, with the Corvette production lines crammed into a rather decrepit old building in which the sports cars stood out like vehicles from a future century.

The production process at St Louis started with the welding up of the steel 'birdcage' which forms the frame of the passenger compartment on T-

31 July 1981, the last St Louis Corvette. Both plants built cars during June and July

CHAPTER SIX

1 June 1981, the first Bowling Green Corvette. Most of the early cars from the new plant were two-tone

topped cars. Once painted, this was fitted to a jig and the individual body panels built up onto it, using a chemical curing bonding agent.

The bonding agent was mixed up in white paper cones and heated up while it cured. The multitude of joints in the body were then sanded by hand and filled to obtain a perfect finish prior to painting. Up until 1976 this filler was asbestos based. To protect the health of the assembly line workers the filler was changed to a new type which unfortunately shrank in service. The effect of this is particularly noticeable on original 1977 cars, where a shallow

1981 engine installed in chassis awaits its body

Painted body receives glass and wiring

CHAPTER SIX

Body drop. Rear bumper is fixed along top only, held out with a temporary stay to clear inner bumper bar

Final inspection at Bowling Green. Each day, samples of the previous day's production are selected at random and every aspect of the car is checked. Monitored results are relayed to the relevant work station

depression forms just below the tops of the front and rear wings where the upper and lower sections are joined. During 1978 the problem was solved with a more stable filler material.

On soft bumpered cars a polyurethane based paint was used for the bumpers. These were painted in a separate part of the plant, and arrived at their fitting station in computer controlled order so that they matched the bodies as they arrived from the paint area. Here the cars had been filled, baked and then wet sanded. Then they were primed, finished and baked again. Meanwhile on the chassis production line the front and rear suspension assemblies, which had arrived in a built-up form, were fastened to the chassis also brought in from outside. These were installed with the frame upside down to simplify assembly. The engine/gearbox units arrived complete with carburettor, water pump and starter motor and were then dropped onto the chassis, by now turned the right way up again. The chassis then proceeded along the production line receiving components such as body mounts, clutch parts and brake and fuel lines. Meanwhile the body was being given its interior fitments, instruments, electrical system and all the other hundreds of parts that go to make a complete Corvette, as it travelled on a cradle through the individual fitting bays.

Finally the body was dropped onto the chassis and the body mounting bolts fastened. Then the wheels and tyres were installed and the car was lowered onto the ground, supporting its own weight. Fluids were added as appropriate, and brake circuit filled and bled in seconds with a vacuum filler. The car was then started by a tester and checked out on a rolling road. This same tester carried out his own alignment and under-car check, sitting on a cushion which he carried from car to car, since the seats had not yet been installed. When the tester was satisfied that the car was running

CHAPTER SIX

properly, it went onto the interior trimming line where door panels, interior trim and seats were fitted as the last stage of the production process. Now the car was driven away and water penetration tested, after which it underwent a final inspection, with remedial work as necessary.

Much to the surprise of those who predicted that General Motors would abandon their limited production sports car, it was announced that assembly would move in 1981 to Bowling Green, Kentucky, 325 miles south east of St Louis and 500 south of Detroit. General Motors bought an old air con-

There are now Corvette shows and rallies all over the United States, Europe and even in Australia

This is the McDorman Show at Columbus, Ohio

ditioning equipment factory of more than half a million square feet, gutted it, extended it and dedicated it to the manufacture of Corvettes.

The contrast with St Louis is astonishing. Bowling Green is a country town with little heavy industry or big city problems and the plant on I-65 provides an ideal and spacious working environment. Further it is thoroughly up to date, apart from a complete lack of robots. Perhaps these will be used on the next generation of Corvettes.

GMAD has made enormous efforts to improve quality at Bowling Green, and many aspects of the production process have been improved. For example, cars are no longer driven finished to the water test, but are taken through it on the production line before carpets are fitted. This has eliminated the St

CHAPTER SIX

Twenty five years of used instrument panels at an American 'flea market'

Louis problem of water and sealer stained carpets. Quality control is now taken extremely seriously at every stage of production and every day eight cars are taken at random from the shipping yard and checked in minute detail. Findings are reported and discussed every morning at a meeting in the brilliantly lit quality area, and then relayed back to each assembly station. Now that performance is no longer the prime reason for buying a Corvette, quality of finish has become a major selling point. Everyone at Bowling Green is aware that while this may be a purpose built Corvette plant it could be converted in a few weeks to the assembly of Citations or Caprices!

Chapter 7
1978-79;
Metamorphosis...

The first 1978 I ever saw was in El Paso, Texas in September 1977. I was driving across the States for a holiday with my brother, and we were headed that day for the Desert Air Museum at Pima and Frank Lloyd Wright's Taliesin West at Scottsdale. We were eating a breakfast of pancake and sausage at a window seat in a Waffle House when it drove into the car park and parked in the brilliant sunshine right beside us. The car was all black with a white interior and immediately attracted a small crowd of admirers. I realized at that moment that the Corvette had a future as well as a past, that the boring trend of the last three years had been reversed.

If the years 1975–77 were years of non-progress and just adequate development every September to show that someone there knew that the car still existed, then 1978 was a year of sensational change and enormous improvement to the car which resulted in the Corvette's acceptance by a wider market, increased sales and the final transformation from a sports to a grand touring theme.

This change was the introduction of the big back window, which had a dramatic effect not only on appearance but also on the interior spaciousness. I think this modification should have been introduced in 1973, though I accept that Chevrolet had their reasons for not doing this. The dark and

The 1978 big back window was the most significant styling change for ten years and gave the body style an extra five years of life

congested interior was suddenly light and spacious, you could take a Corvette on a Continental holiday without thinking about water-proofing the suitcases on the luggage rack, while in daily use it was now a pleasure to put shopping and even household pets into the rear compartment. Along with this tremendous improvement in interior space. Chevrolet resisted the temptation to incorporate token rear seats for legless dwarfs, a trap which contributed to the demise of the Jaguar E type coupé. It has always been vital to the Corvette's image that it is strictly a two seater, 'just you and me, honey' and the two seats make a strong personal statement about the driver which is in direct contrast to the image of the four seater.

A black roller blind was mounted at the top rear of the compartment; this can be pulled across the luggage area to protect the contents from prying eyes and bright sunshine. An unsatisfactory side effect of the new rear glass was that road noise from the rear suspension which had penetrated the thin fibreglass floor was reflected directly forward to the driver. Indeed, these cars have an entirely different acoustic feel to their predecessors.

Also banished forever was the pathetic door panel design of 1969–77, to be replaced by a flat panel with a separate strong arm-rest secured to the steel inner skin of the door by three strong screws. Not since 1964 had a Corvette had such a workmanlike arm-rest, this one incorporating a standard GM plunger for the optional power door locks. 1978 was the first year for these, which are operated by switches on either door and not by the door key as in central locking systems. Advantage was taken of the new rear open space to offer dual rear speakers, and citizens band radio was offered as an integrated unit.

Ahead of the driver, the central console was the same as 1977's but the speedometer and tachometer were all new, set in a new square cut housing. To remove any of the instruments, don't try and undo all those nice exposed Allen head screws, they are fakes! An easily accessible trip reset push knob penetrated the speedo glass, replacing the rather hard to reach wind-up knob of previous years, and the windscreen wiper switch was back on the dashboard in the best American tradition. In front of the passenger was a real glove box, the first on a Corvette since 1967 and on tape-player-equipped

Silver Anniversary edition celebrated 25 years of Corvette production. Accent stripes were adhesive tape. This was the first full dual-coloured Corvette

CHAPTER SEVEN

1978–79; METAMORPHOSIS...

cars it contained dividers for storing tapes. Unfortunately, the lid was held in place by that frightful glove locker twist knob fitted to most American GM cars over the last 10 years, and the one on a 1981 Corvette is just as unreliable as the one on my old 1971 Cadillac Eldorado convertible!

1978 was the 25th anniversary of Corvette production and Chevrolet celebrated this by offering the B2Z Silver Anniversary paint. This was the first dual tone paint option since 1962, with a light silver top half and dark silver bottom half, divided by adhesive dark silver transfers. Approximately one third of all production was made up of these cars, which are thus the commonest of the run. They came with sports mirrors and aluminium wheels as standard, and were heavily advertized in a nationwide bill-board poster campaign featuring a superb side view photograph of the Silver Anniversary car. All 1978 Corvettes have the 'anniversary' front and rear badges which are not therefore signs of a

Opposite *Interior of '78 was a great improvement over previous years. Centre armrest is padded, passenger has glove locker. Door panels are much more durable than previous years and have space for power door lock motors*

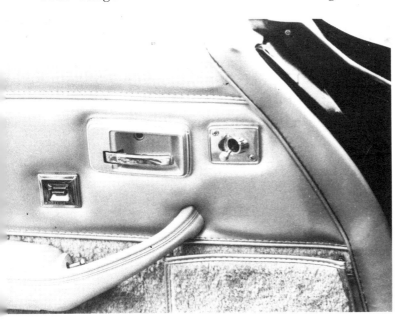

Front of '78 door panel showing power door lock switch, remote mirror joystick and door map pocket

CHAPTER SEVEN

1978 speedometer and tachometer. Push knob resets trip odometer. Centre warning light is for headlight main beam

Internally lit vanity mirror on passenger side visor was new for 1979

resprayed special edition.

The 1978 Corvette was also chosen as the official Indianapolis pace car to supervise the warming up lap of the annual 500 race with its traditional flying start. Like every manufacturer whose car is chosen as a pace car, Chevrolet ran off a special limited edition replica and this was one of the finest Corvettes produced up to that time. Besides being 'loaded' with almost every available option, it featured the new seats with plastic moulded base that were to be standardized in 1979. These tilted halfway up their back and allegedly incorporate an inertia locking device which I have yet to see demonstrated. They are much more comfortable than previous seats. In the Pace Car these were finished in silver leather; the rest of the interior of the car was also silver, an option previously available in 1974 and 1975. Standard on the Pace Car and subsequently to become optional on all Corvettes were the glass reflective roofs, laminated from two sheets of glass. These were mentioned in the 1977 catalogue but never offered. These glass roofs do not fit as well as the standard fibreglass type and always stand proud at the back. In daily use they crack far too readily with only slightly careless use, and are popular as a means of entry by thieves requiring access to the stereo system. Since two roof panels cost almost as much as a brand new engine, city-dwelling Corvette owners either stay with the standard roofs or choose an aftermarket installation, which is cheaper and made of almcst unbreakable Lexan.

At front and rear the Pace Car was fitted with spoilers which were to become an option in 1979. Both spoilers are bolt on and semi-rigid, the front being a three-piece affair with a soft centre-section, ingeniously arranged to hinge upwards when it contacts the road over major bumps. The spoilers were claimed to give a half mpg improvement in fuel

CB radio was optional 1978 onwards. GM passenger car heater and air conditioning control unit replaced the nice knurled wheels control in 1977

consumption, and they do seem to make the front of the car lift less at speeds in excess of 100 mph. Fast driving European owners have reported that the front spoiler diminishes the air flow into the front brakes and leads to premature fade, a problem also observed with the new shaped '80 and '81 cars. Also a new option for 1978 was a wider 60 profile tyre. This had a nominal section of 255/60 as opposed to

CHAPTER SEVEN

104

1978–79; METAMORPHOSIS . . .

the standard 225/70 and while it looks tremendous it is less than satisfactory on rough corners, white lines and road irregularities taken fast. Worst of all, these tyres tend to aquaplane about 20 mph sooner than equivalent 70 profile 'boots' on heavily puddled roads.

The 1979 Corvette used the new plastic based bucket seats introduced on the 1978 Pace Car,

Pace Car replica had front and rear spoilers, glass roofs and silver leather interior. Car became an instant classic

The Corvette was chosen to pace the warm-up lap at the 1978 Indianapolis 500 race

1979 Corvette had new seats and 1977 front and rear badges. This is a GM press release picture, production cars had rear window moulding painted matt black

CHAPTER SEVEN

L-48 350 installed in 1978 car. Cold air for the engine has been drawn from ahead of radiator since 1976. This was second year for co-axial AC compressor, at the right of the fan, and optional cruise control servo just beyond the distributor cover

available in leather or cloth finish. Other Pace Car features offered as options were the glass roof panels and the front and rear spoilers which were painted body colour to match the car. Due to a change in Federal car lighting regulations, halogen high beam headlight units were now permitted and fitted. These had previously emitted too much light to comply with the regulations. 1977-style crossed flags replaced the 'anniversary' front and rear badges. The car was more popular than ever, this being the first model year in which production exceeded 50,000 units.

Chapter 8
1980-82;
...For a new age

By 1980 the original 1968 body shape had managed 12 years of production and while there had been a number of changes during that time, Chevrolet was still making basically the same car. Most of the components on the car and the majority of the body panels were still interchangeable.

But the GM stylists still had some tricks in reserve to wring another three years out of the old body and chassis. The changes they made for 1980 not only improved the appearance but reduced the drag co-efficient (Cd) from 0.500 to below 0.450.

The new nose featured a full width front spoiler integrated into the soft bumper, which now extended right round to the front of the wheels. Incorporated into the soft nose were new side marker lamps and cornering lights which lit the road to the side of the car when the indicator switch was depressed and the lights on. Cornering lights like these had been used on the Cadillac for many years, but this was the first time they had been incorporated on a Corvette. A deep black rubber extension piece was fitted to the underside of the spoiler on the soft nose to give it a flexible extension and a steel skid was incorporated to protect the spoiler on full spring-compression.

The lower lip of the front grille extended out further from the upper lip, making the car look still longer and lower. At the rear, an all new soft

bumper incorporated new tail lights and an integral spoiler and, at last, the little black overriders on the bumpers front and rear were abandoned. Air conditioning was now standard, as were dual remote control external sport mirrors, power windows and a tilt-telescopic steering wheel.

The L-82 engine was now available only with automatic transmission due to emission certification problems, while a special engine of only 305 cubic inch (5.0 litres) capacity was introduced for California, with its stricter emission laws. I almost omitted this engine capacity from the sub-title of this book because I see it as a boring variation on the 350 to meet a legal requirement, and not as an exciting engine in its own right.

1980 Corvettes were approximately 250 pounds lighter than '79s and this was of tremendous

Opposite *'An automobile of which at least half the length is hood'*—Michael Sedgwick's definition of a classic, from his Cars of the Thirties and Forties

The new rear bumper moulding for 1980 incorporated a spoiler. Thankfully, the 1975–79 black overiders are gone

CHAPTER EIGHT

The first 300 Corvettes ever made were white. Just as Ferraris should be Ferrari red, so the colour for Corvettes is Corvette white

Opposite The new 1980 shovel nose was soft right back to the wheels. Lower side marker light is a direction indicator

significance; the cars had been getting gradually heavier since 1968. Great savings were achieved throughout by reducing the thickness of the bonnet, doors and roof panels, and fitting thinner glass to windscreen and side windows. The most significant weight reduction, however, was in the support structure for the new soft nose, which was fibreglass rather than steel, and in a new aluminium differential and support crossmember.

The new differential was very similar to the previous cast iron design, and trimmed away weight from the back where the car was grossly overweight. While all the weight saving was aimed at reducing fuel consumption it has also improved the

CHAPTER EIGHT

1981 was externally unchanged apart from front and rear badges

handling considerably, and the difference is easily perceived from the driver's seat.

Further improvements on the 1980 were a new lower profile bonnet noticeably lighter than the 1979's, and plastic trim in the side vent louvres. Another long overdue improvement was the incorporation of the two glove boxes behind the passenger seat into one, with a new hard plastic drop-in section to cover the jack. An illuminated vanity mirror was incorporated on the passenger side sun visor, a feature which would have been unthinkable in the Corvettes of 15 years before.

Federal regulations still continued to spoil the Corvette, for 1980 models it was an 85 mph speedo which also incorporated a stop to prevent the needle going 'off the clock'. Luckily, a 1979 speedometer can be incorporated if required, though the tachometer must also be changed for a perfect match.

A new feature was an optional roof panel carrier which was assembled solely for carrying the roof panel, and which clipped into holes in the rear deck of the car. It is an ungainly system and I have never yet seen it in use on the road.

A new one piece rear badge spelt Corvette in lower case upright letters, and a matching badge fixed to the otherwise plain front wing identified L-82 models.

The final overall weight reduction achieved over a similarly equipped 1979 model was 235 lb. The engineers knew that if the Corvette was to continue, and not be an embarrassment to the Corporation, then further weight savings and fuel economy improvements would have to be introduced for 1981.

Externally the 1981 carried different crossed flag badges at front and rear. The side trim mouldings which run between the wheels below the door were all-black rather than black and silver anodized.

The weight saving was not enormous, only 17 lb

1980–82; . . . FOR A NEW AGE

Another factory shot of the 1981 Corvette. External changes were confined to the badges

CHAPTER EIGHT

Power seat was new option for 1981

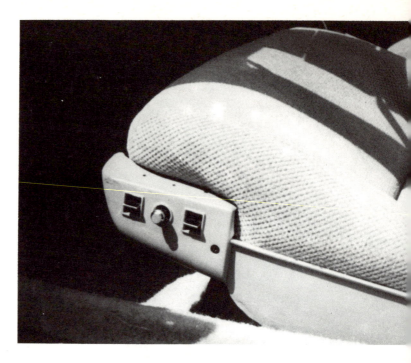

1980–82 roof panel carrier

over the 1980 type, but a considerable amount of emission equipment had been added. The brilliant new weight saving device was a fibreglass rear spring. It was 33 lb lighter than the multi-leaf steel spring which it replaced, a design that had been used with a varying number of leaves since 1963. It reduced the rear end weight yet again, and gave a better ride since there was no interleaf friction. This friction has always been a problem with earlier Corvettes since the plastic separators inserted between the steel leaves during manufacture wear through within the first two years of service.

The new rear spring was exhibited in the US pavilion at the 1982 World Fair in Knoxville, the first Corvette component to achieve this distinction! For reasons never made clear the conventional spring was retained for 1981 cars fitted with manual transmissions or 'gymkhana' suspension options.

Weight savings were also made on the newly designated L-81 engine. These consisted of a lightweight aluminium intake manifold, tubular exhaust manifolds to replace the heavy but efficient cast iron 'rams horns', and finned magnesium valve covers similar to those used previously on the L-82 engines. The L-82 engine was dropped and the L-81 certified for California so there were now no optional engines.

To achieve the economies required, the engine was fitted with an electronic control module (ECM), to adjust the ignition timing of a new distributor and the air-fuel mixture of an electro mechanical carburettor. The ECM is fed by sensors around the engine and in the catalytic converter. These devices enabled the engine to run more economically on a weaker air/fuel mixture, and thus reduce emissions. At the same time they make it much harder for the home mechanic to tune his own engine or discard his catalytic converter.

1982 'Cross-fire' fuel injection, and optional dual-colour paint and glass roof panels

CHAPTER EIGHT

The automatic transmission was now fitted with a locking clutch torque converter which mechanically locked the drive through the converter in second and third gears, so contributing further to fuel economy. New rear axle ratios made the car even more long legged with a 2.72 for the four speed and 2.87 for the automatic. All 1980s were fitted with a 3.07:1 axle.

Inside the car three new options were offered. The first was a six-way power driver's seat, not quite the kind of thing one likes to see in a sports car, but a boon for short drivers and no worse than the unpowered seat for tall ones.

A self seeking radio was offered as well with LED time display, and when this was fitted the clock was replaced by an oil temperature gauge. Instead of the standard door mounted controls for the sport mirrors, powered door mirrors with a joy stick

1982 Collectors Edition special aluminium wheels

1982 Cross-fire injection engine. One circular air filter serves each bank of the V8 engine

control on the centre console could be ordered as an option.

Towards the end of the 1981 model year, on 1 June, Corvette production moved to the new plant at Bowling Green, Kentucky. To celebrate the millions of dollars that had been spent in the paint section of the new facility, a new dual colour option was introduced. Above the waist line light colours were offered, with striping on the bonnet moulding matching the darker bottom half. Production continued in parallel at the two plants during June and July. The last Corvette to leave St Louis—on 31

CHAPTER EIGHT

Half a million dollars worth of '82s lined up in November 1982 at a Fort Lauderdale, Florida Chevrolet dealer. In 1967, '67s were just as plentiful, now they are sought after as the last of the old style cars

July—was white with beige interior.

For 1982 the engine was changed again, this time for the better, with a higher 9:1 compression ratio and electronic fuel injection. Corvettes had had fuel injection before. It was offered from 1957 to 1965 on the Small Block V8, but the latest system uses just two injectors, one per bank of cylinders. Known as throttle body injection (TBI) it actually improved horsepower to 200, 10 per cent up on 1981. Better control of the air/fuel mixture allowed the use of a 9:1 compression ratio which contributes towards

Collectors Edition 1982 in Dearborn, Michigan

the extra power. The under bonnet appearance was improved, too, with finned valve covers peeping out from beneath the injector cover which carries the words 'cross fire injection' in Corvette script. The same script on the body side identifies all 1982s.

Not only was the power increased but the fuel consumption improvement was dramatic. While it's hard to improve on 20 miles per Imperial gallon on a

CHAPTER EIGHT

long fast run in a carburetted Corvette, better than 25 mpg has been reported with the 1982 cars.

An all new 4-speed overdrive automatic transmission is fitted to all 1982 Corvettes; there is no manual transmission option. This gearbox has a locking torque converter in second, third and fourth gears, and at 70 mph in top gear the engine is running at only 1600 rpm compared to a typical 3500 rpm for a Small Block equipped 1968!

1982 is intended to be the last year of production for the Corvette with this body style, and at the time of writing there are broad hints that the new model will be considerably different. To mark the end of this particular line Chevrolet introduced a Collectors Edition priced at a basic $22,537. This features a very special interior, silver leather seats with contrast panels and adjustable backs, and virtually every option. The big rear window introduced in 1978 was converted to a hatchback for the Collector's Edition only. It is a superb option, and in spite of being frameless has caused little problem with leaks and squeaks. Externally the silver-beige metallic paint has special transfers and pin stripes, and special Collectors Edition badges are fitted. Aluminium wheels with radial fins and special hubs are reminiscent of the 1967's optional equipment.

Who would have predicted back in 1968 that 14 years later the same model would be such a different car, so much quieter, so much more economical, and that the total production run from 1968 to 1982 would exceed half a million?

Notes on American model years

Whilst in Europe we accept the date of first registration as the nominal manufacture date of the car, a system emphasised in Great Britain since 1963 by the use of the suffix letters for registration, American cars are always identified by their year of manufacture or *model year*.

The system started because American manufacturers have traditionally facelifted their cars every year, and any year of American car, be it a Corvette, Thunderbird or Chrysler, will have specific characteristics relating only to that year. A number or a letter in the *vehicle identification number* (VIN) identifies it as that year.

The model year is four months out of phase with the calendar year. For example a 1978 Corvette, the first with the big back window and the last with the low hinged seat, might have been manufactured anytime from the beginning of September 1977, when the assembly plant re-opened after retooling, to mid-summer 1978 when it would have closed for the annual holiday of the assembly line workers and the re-tooling for the 1979 models. Since demand is usually at its highest with the announcement of the new facelifted model at the beginning of the model year, approximately one third of the 1978 models will actually have been made during calendar 1977. For example a 1978 Corvette with a base engine (and not one of the special Pace Cars) would typically have had a serial number IZ87L8S412345. The sixth digit, being an 8, denotes the model year; 1978.

While the whole system originated from the manufacturers' attempts to persuade the public to buy a new car every year, it also means that prices must be reduced by dealers every summer to get rid of unsold stocks. This is clearly a far better system from the consumers' view point. In Europe, even a knowledgeable buyer can buy a new car with only delivery mileage on the clock which may have been rusting in a field for up to three years prior to delivery to the dealer.

The identifying marks on Corvettes are covered in depth in the *Corvette Black Book* published by Michael Bruce Associates. The VIN numbers are fully explained along with engine suffix letters.

Corvette owners wishing to find out more about the manufacture date, options and original supplying dealer of their car should locate one of the computer print outs which, depending on year, are variously positioned between tachometer and speedometer bodies, in the strut rod support location bracket beneath of the differential and, on all models, fixed to the top of the fuel tank.

Any year of Corvette can be identified at a glance without referring to its VIN number by reference to the following *significant* changes to basically equipped cars.

1968   New body style
1969   New rear lights, ignition switch on column, 350 small block
1970   New front and side grilles, big block now 454, square exhausts
1971   Reduced compressions, last light monitors, no headlight washers
1972   Burglar alarm standard, no light monitors
1973   New soft nose
1974   New soft tail and last 454

1975 Revised soft nose and soft tail, HEI and catalytic exhaust, last convertible
1976 Vega 4-spoke steering wheel, no ventilation grilles on rear deck
1977 New padded steering wheel and new centre instrument binnacle
1978 New back window, door panels, speedometer and tachometer
1979 New high hinged plastic based seats
1980 New aerodynamic soft nose and tail
1981 L-81 engine, 3 speed auto with locking converter, last 4 speed
1982 Cross fire injection badges, TBI, 4 speed automatic with locking converter.

Referring to the VIN number we have the following:

Corvette model identification data

YEAR	VIN	YEAR	VIN	YEAR	VIN
1953	3	1963	3	1973	3
1954	4	1964	4	1974	4
1955	5	1965	5	1975	5
1956	6	1966	6	1976	6
1957	7	1967	7	1977	7
1958	8	1968	8	1978	8
1959	9	1969	9	1979	9
1960	0	1970	0	1980	A
1961	1	1971	1	1981	B
1962	2	1972	2	1982	C

Specifications

Basic dimensions	1968	1982
Overall length	15 ft $2\frac{1}{4}$ in.	15 ft $5\frac{1}{2}$ in.
Overall width	5 ft $9\frac{1}{4}$ in.	5 ft $9\frac{1}{4}$ in.
Overall height	3 ft $11\frac{3}{4}$ in.	4 ft 0 in.
Track, front	58.3 in.	58.7 in.
Track, rear	59.0 in.	59.5 in.
Wheelbase	98.0 in.	98.0 in.
Kerb weight	3425 lb	3342 lb
Price	$4663.00	$18,290.07

Small Block engines

RPO no.	Capacity (cu. in.)	Bore/stroke (in.)	cr:1	Max. bhp	Available year	
LG-4	305	$3\frac{47}{64} \times 3\frac{31}{64}$	8.5	180*	'80 (California only)	
—	327	$4 \times 3\frac{1}{4}$	10.5	300	'68	
L-79	327	$4 \times 3\frac{1}{4}$	11.0	350	'68	
—	350	$4 \times 3\frac{31}{64}$	10.25	300	'69	'70
L-46	350	$4 \times 3\frac{31}{64}$	11.0	350	'69	'70
LT-1	350	$4 \times 3\frac{31}{64}$	11.0	370	'70	
—	350	$4 \times 3\frac{31}{64}$	8.5	270	'71	'72
LT-1	350	$4 \times 3\frac{31}{64}$	9.0	330	'71	'72
—	350	$4 \times 3\frac{31}{64}$	8.5	195*	'73	'74
L-82	350	$4 \times 3\frac{31}{64}$	9.0	250*	'73	'74

L-48	350	$4 \times 3\frac{31}{64}$	8.5	165*	'75	'76
L-82	350	$4 \times 3\frac{31}{64}$	9.0	205*	'75	'76
L-48	350	$4 \times 3\frac{31}{64}$	8.5	180*	'77	
L-82	350	$4 \times 3\frac{31}{64}$	9.0	220*	'78	
L-48	350	$4 \times 3\frac{31}{64}$	8.5	185*	'78	
L-82	350	$4 \times 3\frac{31}{64}$	9.0	225*	'79	
L-48	350	$4 \times 3\frac{31}{64}$	8.5	190*	'79	'80
L-82	350	$4 \times 3\frac{31}{64}$	9.0	230*	'80	
L-81	350	$4 \times 3\frac{31}{64}$	8.2	180*	'81	
L-83	350	$4 \times 3\frac{31}{64}$	9.0	200*	'82	

*SAE Nett

Big Block engines

RPO no.	Capacity (cu. in.)	Bore/stroke (in.)	cr:1	Max bhp	Available year	
L-36	427	$4\frac{1}{4} \times 3\frac{47}{64}$	10.25	390	'68	'69
L-68	427	$4\frac{1}{4} \times 3\frac{47}{64}$	10.25	400	'68	'69
L-71	427	$4\frac{1}{4} \times 3\frac{47}{64}$	11.0	435	'68	'69
L-88	427	$4\frac{1}{4} \times 3\frac{47}{64}$	12.25	n.a.**	'68	'69
LS-5	454	$4\frac{1}{4} \times 4$	10.25	390	'70	
LS-7	454	$4\frac{1}{4} \times 4$	11.25	460	'70	
LS-5	454	$4\frac{1}{4} \times 4$	8.5	365	'71	'72
LS-6	454	$4\frac{1}{4} \times 4$	9.0	425	'71	
LS-4	454	$4\frac{1}{4} \times 4$	8.25	270*	'73	'74

*SAE Nett
**Probably more than 500 bhp.

Notes: 1972 engines have same output as 1971 but were described for the first time with Nett figures

305 = 5 litres, 327 = 5.361 litres, 350 = 5.738 litres, 427 = 7 litres, 454 = 7.443 litres

Bibliography

There are dozens of Corvette books in print, I list the outstanding ones all of which I have used in the preparation of this book.

Books
Corvette; America's Star Spangled Sports Car, Karl Ludvigsen
   Automobile Quarterly Publications, second edition 1978
The Corvette Black Book (de-luxe edition)
   Michael Bruce Associates Inc., 1980
Corvette; An American Classic
   Petersen Publishing Company, 1978
Corvette; A Piece of the Action, Mitchell & Girdler
   Automobile Quarterly Publications, 1977
Corvette! America's Only
   Michael Bruce Associates Inc., 1978

Periodicals
Vette Vues magazine (monthly)
   Vette Vues, Sandy Springs, Georgia
Corvette News (bi-monthly, now quarterly)
   Chevrolet Motor Division, General Motors Corporation, 1968–82
Annual Corvette sales brochures
   Chevrolet Motor Division, General Motors Corporation, 1968–82

Acknowledgements

Special thanks are due from the author to Ken Jestes, Rhoddy Harvey-Bailey, Becky Bodnor of *Corvette News*, Bill Locke of *Vette Vues* magazine and to Zora Arkus Duntov who is the father of the modern Corvette, also to the Kirks family of Washington DC for their great hospitality on my many American visits.

Many owners were kind enough to lend their cars to photograph including Tony Fisk, Stan Fogo, Anne Foster, Ray Hubbard, Ken Jestes, Sam Pearlman, Bob Williams and thank you to those many Corvette owners on both sides of the Atlantic whose parked cars I have photographed without their knowledge.

The best photographs are by Bill Locke of *Vette Vues* magazine, and those taken by and kindly loaned by *Corvette News*, GM Photographic, Chevrolet Public Relations, GM Public Relations, GM Styling, and GM Assembly Division, Robin Summers Photography, Terry Sims, Jon Barraclough and Dr Seifert. All other photographs by the author.

Index

A
air-conditioning 10, 73, 103
Arkus-Duntov, Zora 61
Australia 24
Automatic transmission 25, 38, 122

B
Barbour suit 19
Bearings, wheel 19, 37–38
Big block engine 10, 23, 31, 36, 41, 61, 84
Bowling Green 83, 86, 91, 123
Brake, calipers 31–33
Brake, parking 33
Bulgaria 11

C
Cadillac 99, 109
California 11, 111, 119
Canada 51, 84
Car and Driver 61
Catalytic convertor 62, 77, 119
Chassis 25, 26, 31
Chevrolet 6, 25, 40, 80, 99
   Camaro 6, 80
   Vega 76
Citroën 54
Clutch 38, 44
Collector's Edition 122, 126
Convertible top 7, 17, 19, 48, 73
Cross-Fire injection 123, 124

D
Defroster, rear 19, 77
Detroit 6, 84
   Grand Prix 6
Differential 25, 38, 112
Door handles 20
Door panels 24, 95, 99
Dream cars 17

E
Earls Court Show 17
East Jefferson Boulevard 6, 24
El Paso, Texas 93
Engines L-82 64, 111, 119
   L-88 23
   LT-1 40, 44, 48, 52, 64
   LS-5 41, 52
   LS-7 44
   ZL-1 20, 23

F
Federal Regulations 49, 57, 60–61, 108, 114
Felton, Northumberland 44
Ferrari 7, 40, 112
Fibreglass 31, 61
Fibre optics 19, 52
Ford 6, 40, 83
Fuel injection 124
Fuel tank 25, 29, 38

G
GMAD 85, 91
Gearbox, manual 30, 38
General Motors 12, 22, 24, 30, 33, 49, 53, 80
Geneva Salon 22

H
Handling 26, 114
Hardtop, detachable 15, 18, 59
Headlights 7, 10, 47, 61
Headlight washers 21
Holley carburettor 44
Honda 51

I
Ignition 40, 62, 119
Ignition, lock 20
Indianapolis 500 101, 104

J
Jaguar 40, 94

K
Kamm 7
Knoxville, Tenn. 119

L
Lexan 101
Louisville, Ky. 6
Luggage rack 19, 51

M
McDorman Show 90
Mako Shark 17, 21
Maserati 40
Mercedes-Benz 41
Mexico 84
Michigan 14
Milford 82, 84
Mitchell, Bill 22
Motor Trend 61
Muncie, Ind. 38

O
Oldsmobile 6
Opel Manta 24

P
Pace Car 101, 105
Pima, Ariz 93
Pontiac 6
   Firebird 6
Porsche 40

R
Radio 14, 78, 122
Right hand drive 24, 110
Rust 31, 77

S
SAE horsepower 52
Saarinen, Eero 84
St Louis 20, 83, 91, 123
Sedgwick, Michael 111
Sidepipes 20, 34
Silicone brake fluid 33
Silver Anniversary 99
Small block engine 23, 28, 31, 40
Spindle, rear 37
Spoilers 101, 109
Spring, rear 25, 119
Steering wheel 20, 76, 79
Stingray/Sting Ray 21, 79
Suspension—front 26, 40
Suspension—rear 27, 29, 40

T
T-Roofs 19, 101, 114, 118
Tail-lights 24
Thieves 15, 101
Thompson, Dick 22
Tonawanda, NY 84
Trailing arms 25, 26
Turbo-Hydramatic 25, 38, 120
Tyres 27, 30, 51, 54, 103

U
Universal joints 40

W
Walker, Wayne 20
Warren, Mich. 14, 84
Wheels 21, 41, 78, 84, 99, 122
Wheels, wide 19, 27, 38
Windscreen wipers 11, 12, 17, 54
Wright, Frank Lloyd 93